Mary was engaged to Joseph. She was getting ready for the day when they would be married.

Luke 1:27

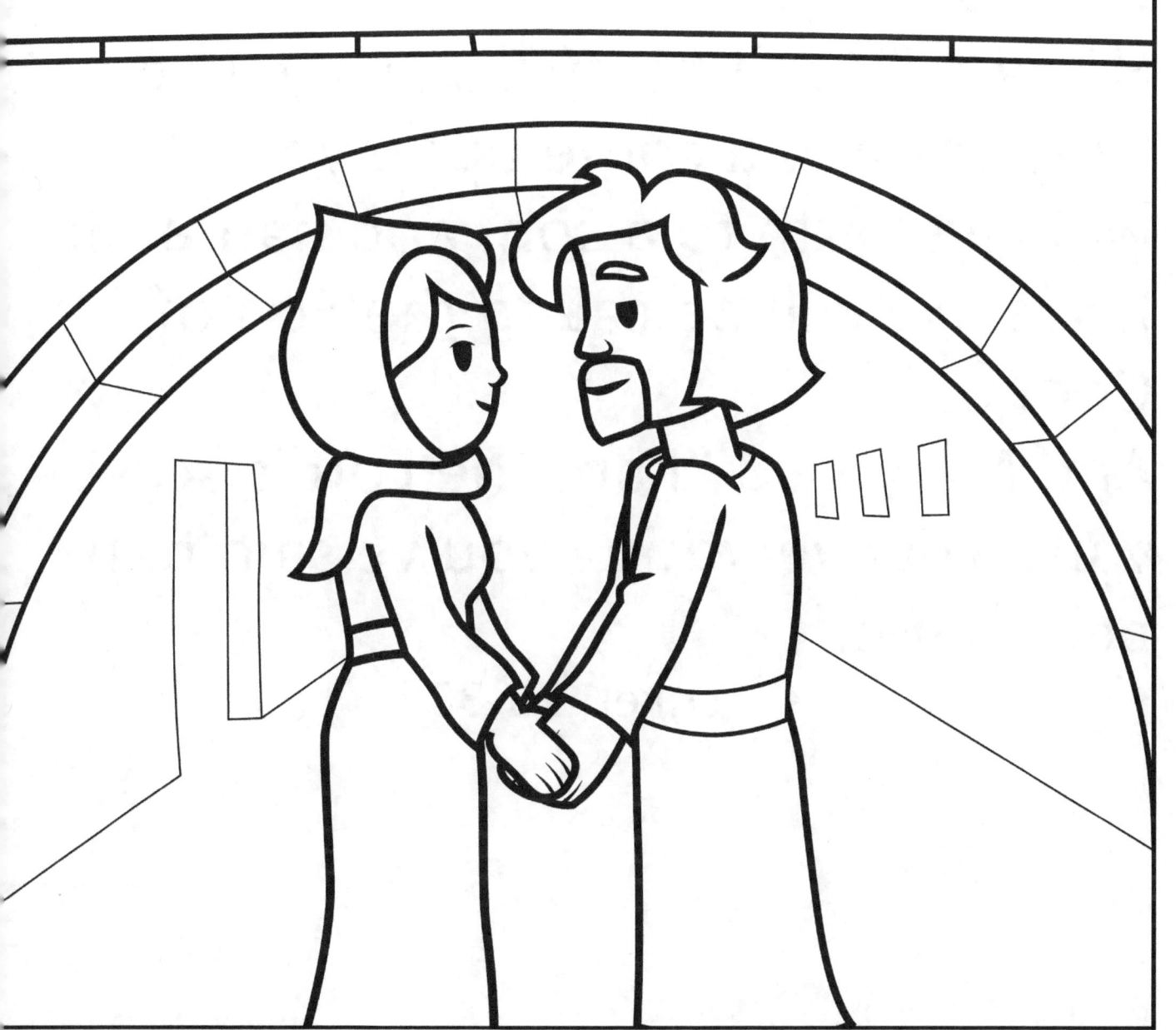

The angel Gabriel was sent from God to Mary.
He said "Don't be afraid Mary. The Holy Spirit will come upon you. You will give birth to a son, and name him Jesus. He will be called the Son of God."
And Mary said "I am the Lord's servant! Let everything you've said happen to me."

Luke 1:26-38

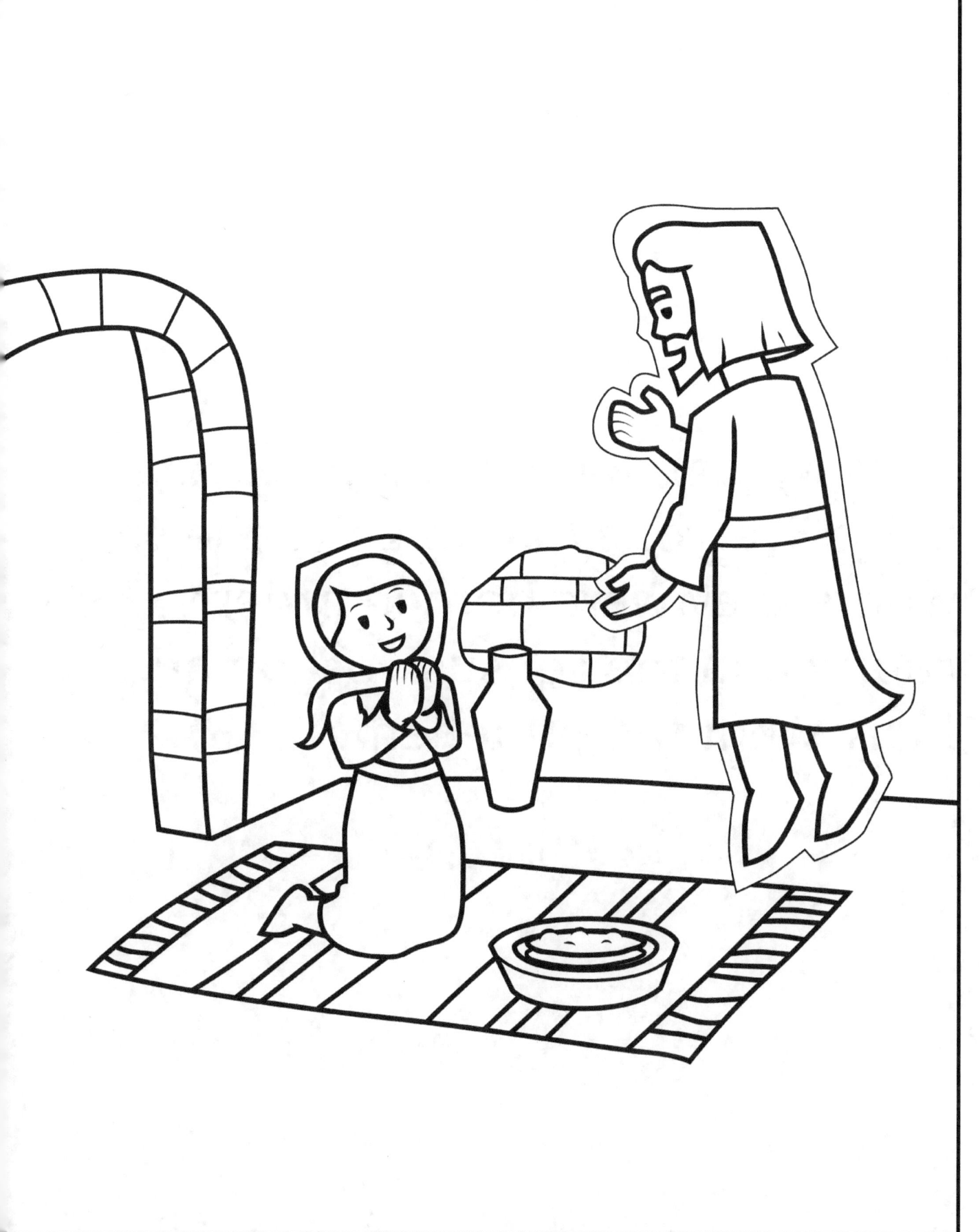

Mary was soon going to have a baby. Everyone had to go to the city where they were born in order to be counted in the census. Joseph and Mary went to Bethlehem.

Luke 2:3-4

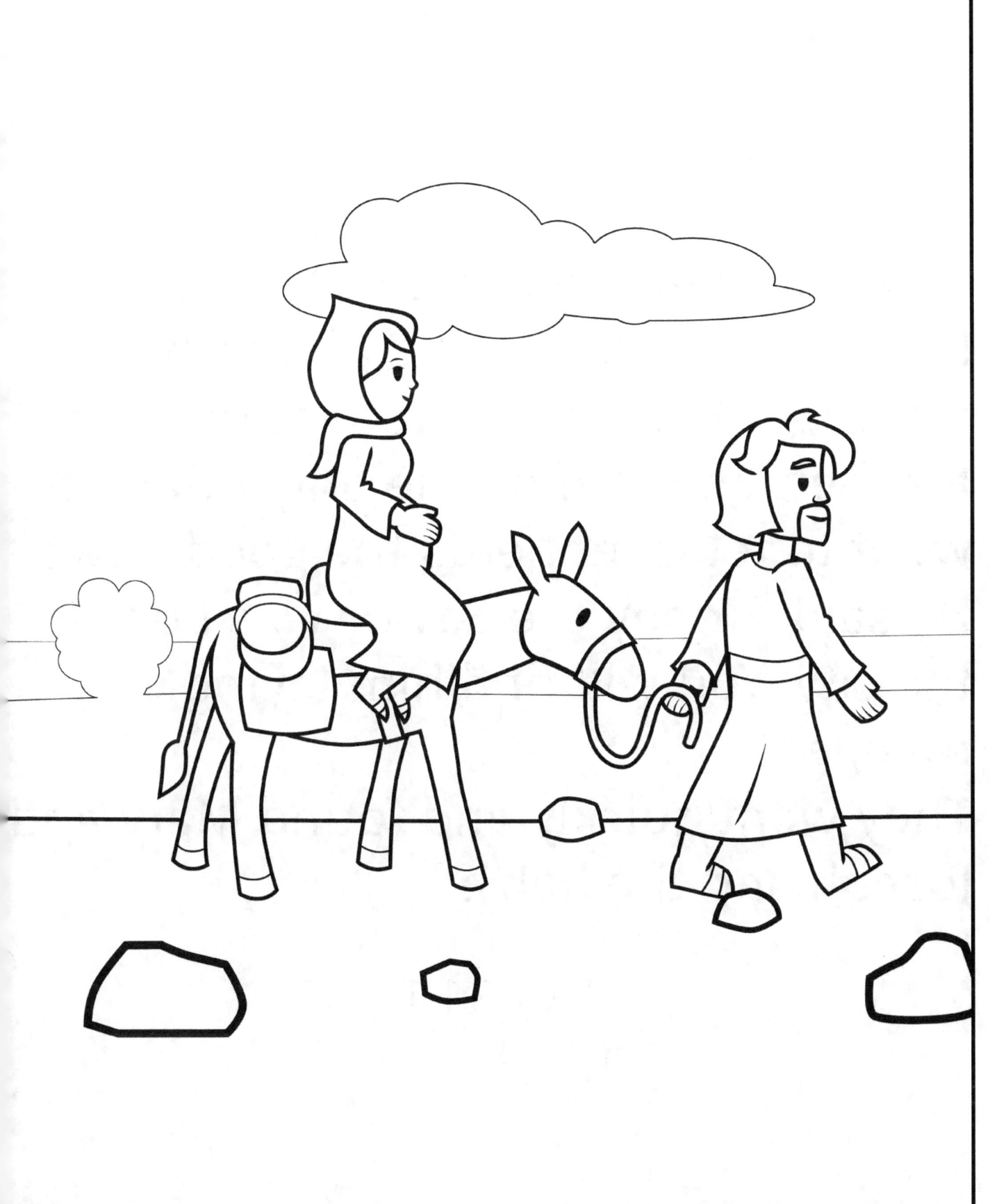

While they were there, Mary's first-born son was born. She placed him in a manger because there was no room for them in the inn. The angel Gabriel went to tell shepherds the good news. He said "Today the Savior was born in the city. You will find him laying in a manger".
They went quickly and found Mary and Joseph and the baby.

Luke 2:1-17

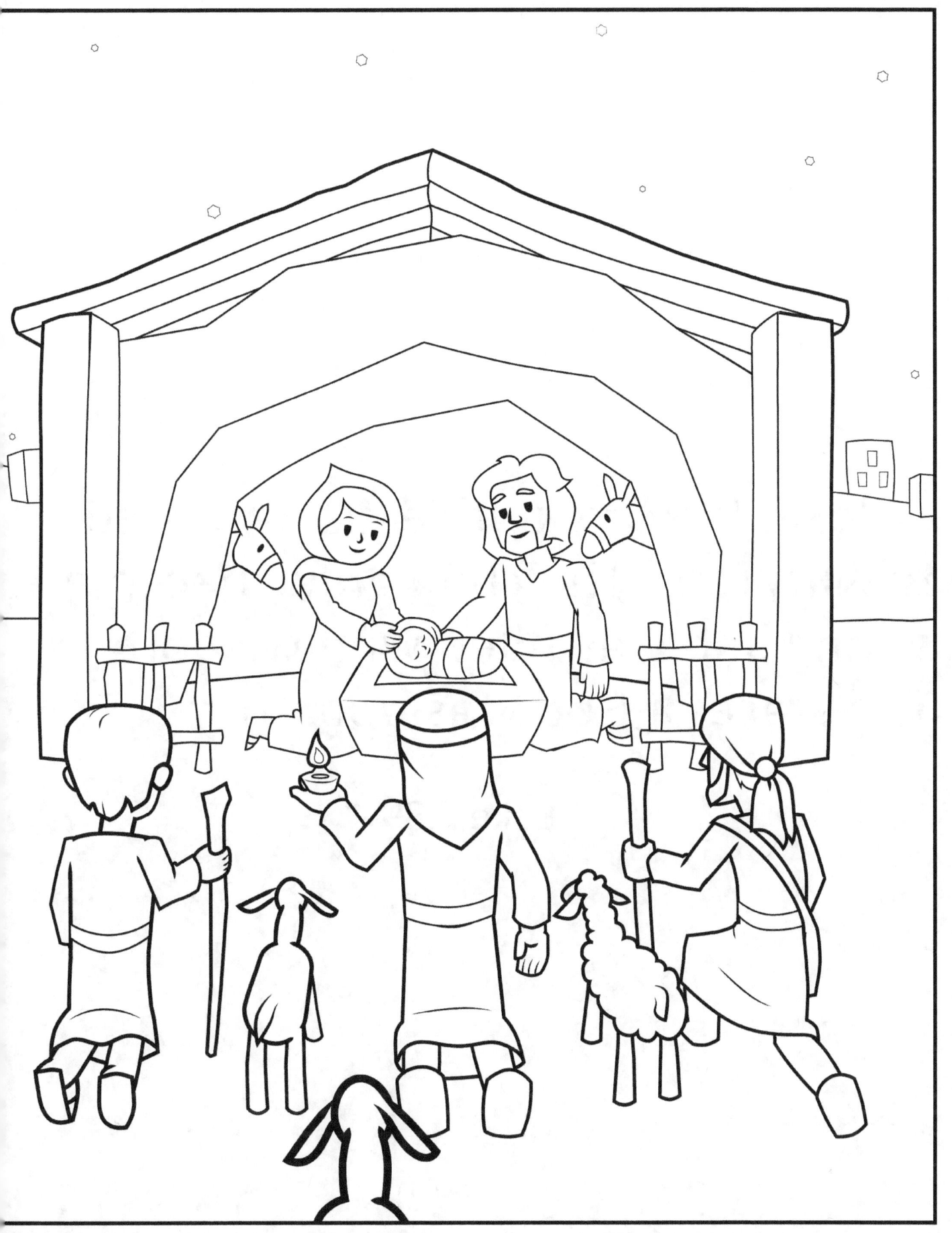

Joseph, Mary and Jesus returned to Nazareth. The child grew, became strong and was filled with wisdom. The grace of God was upon him.

Luke 2:39

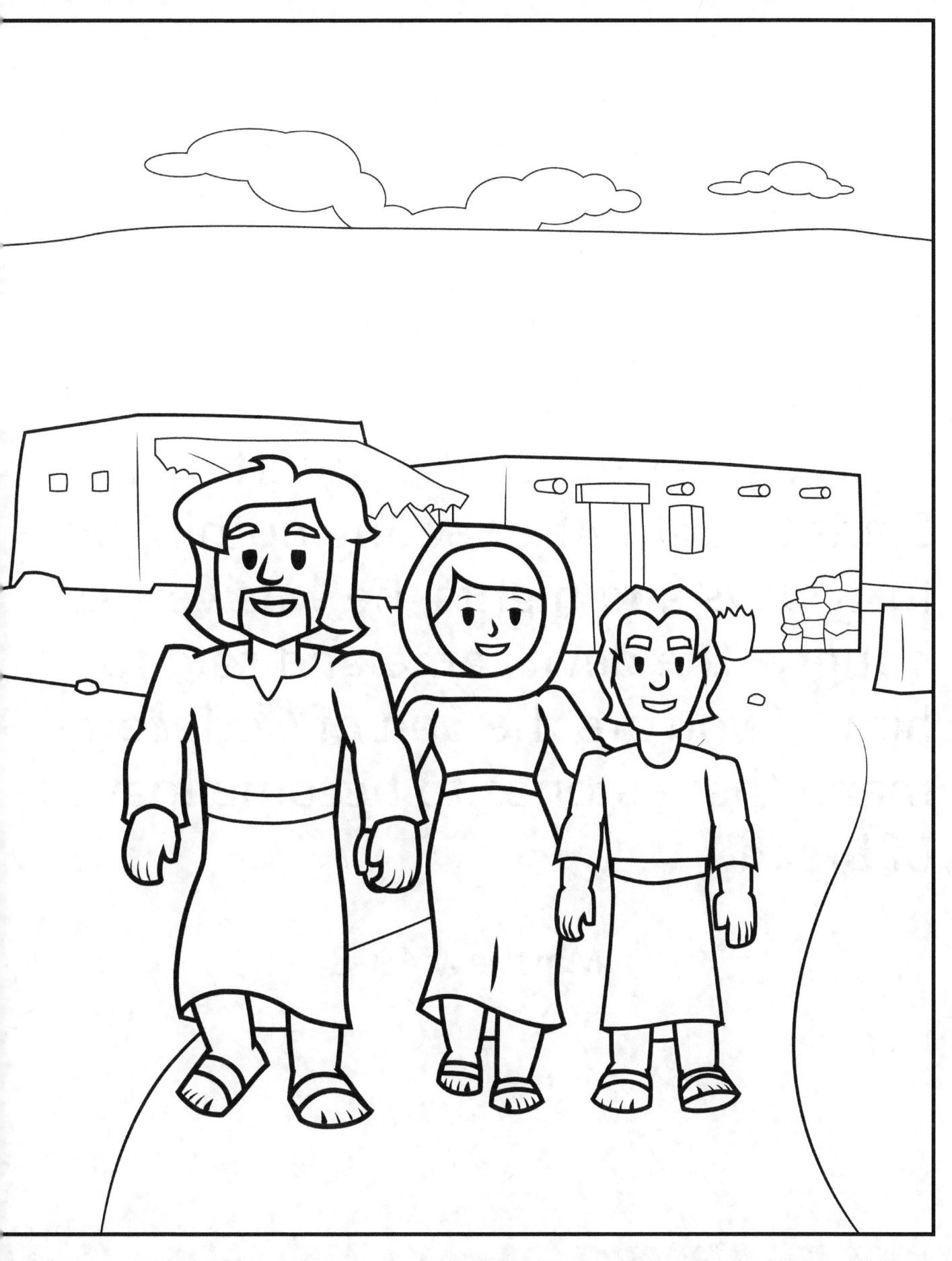

Jesus was led to the desert by the Spirit to pray. After eating nothing for forty days and nights, he was very hungry. The devil came and said to him "If you are the Son of God, command these stones to become loaves of bread".

Matthew 4:1-3

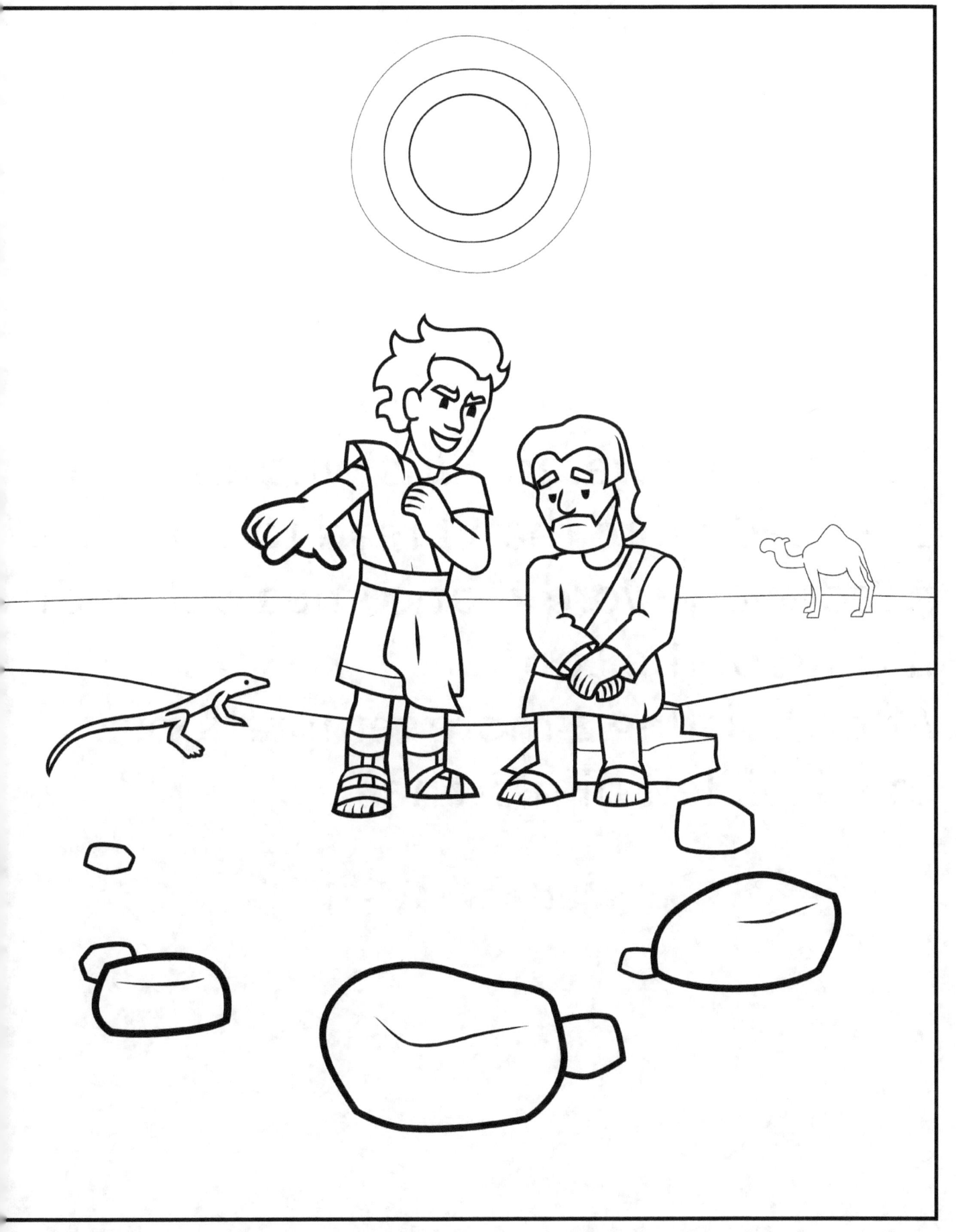

Jesus answered "It is written, "People need more than bread to live–they
need every word that comes out of the
mouth of the Lord.'"
After resisting 2 more temptations...
the devil left him alone.

Matthew 4:4-11

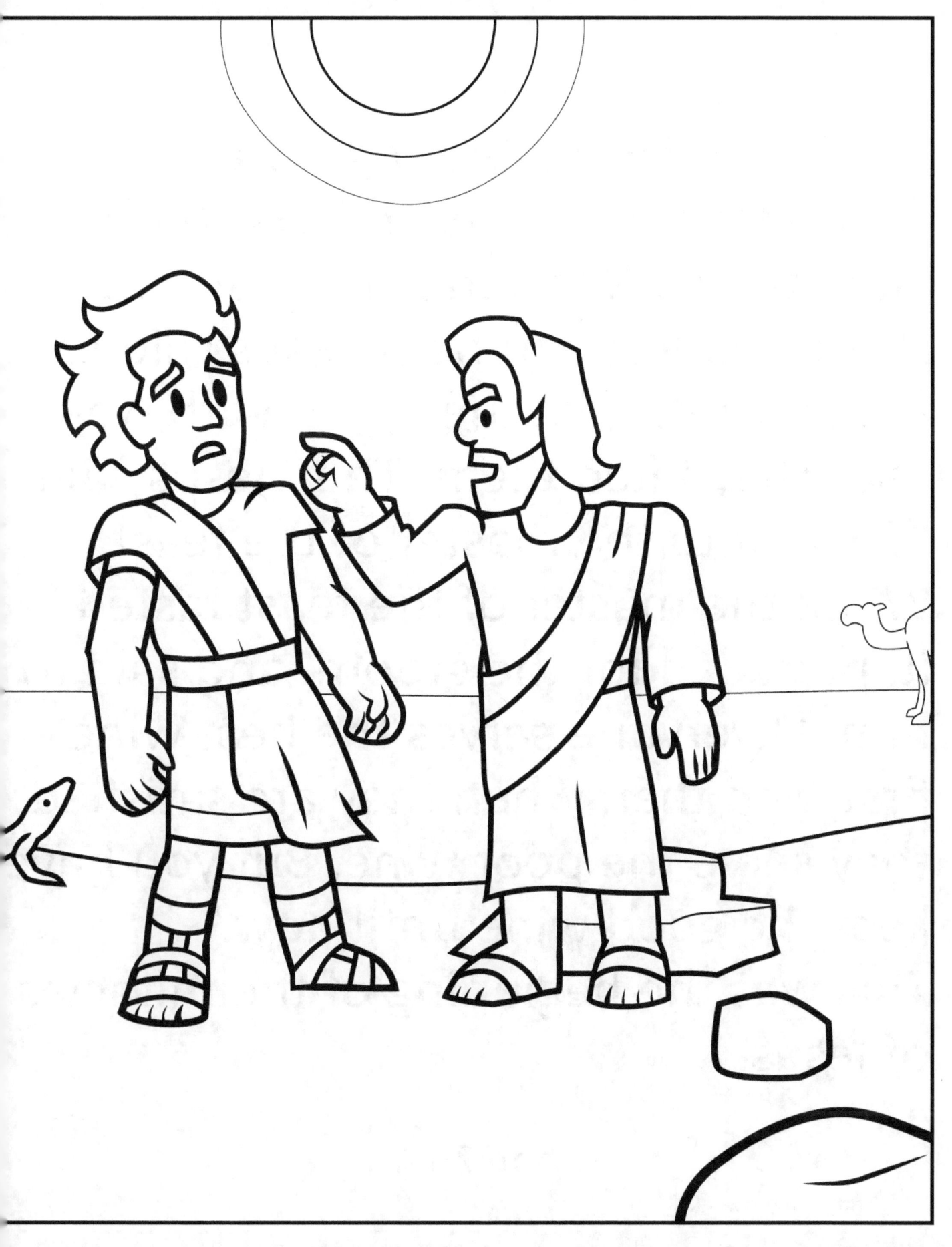

They were celebrating a wedding. Mary and Jesus and his students were there. When the wine ran out she asked Jesus to help. Jesus said to the servants "Fill these jars with water." They filled them. Then Jesus said "Serve it to the master of the feast." When the master of the feast tasted it, he called for the groom, and said to him, "Everyone serves the best wine first, and then when they are satisfied they serve the poor wine. But you have kept the good wine until now."
This was the beginning of the miracles of Jesus.

John 2:1-11

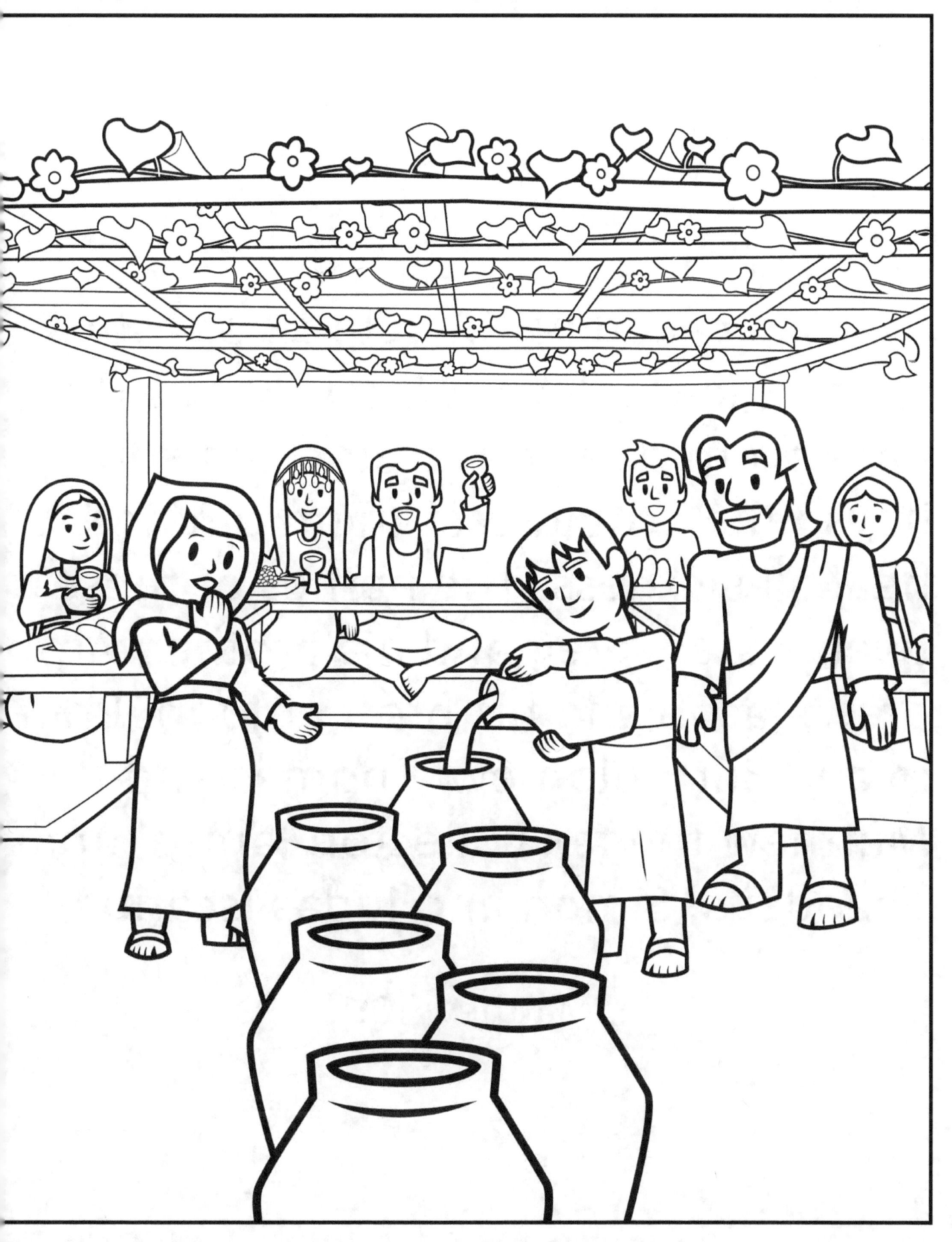

Jesus called his 12 helpers apostles, which means "One Who is Sent". He gave them power over unclean spirits, so they could cast them out and heal all sickness. The names of these twelve are: Peter, and his brother, Andrew; Jacob and his brother John; Philip and Bartholomew, Thomas and Matthew the tax collector; James, and Thaddeus; Simon and Judas Iscariot.

Matthew 10:1

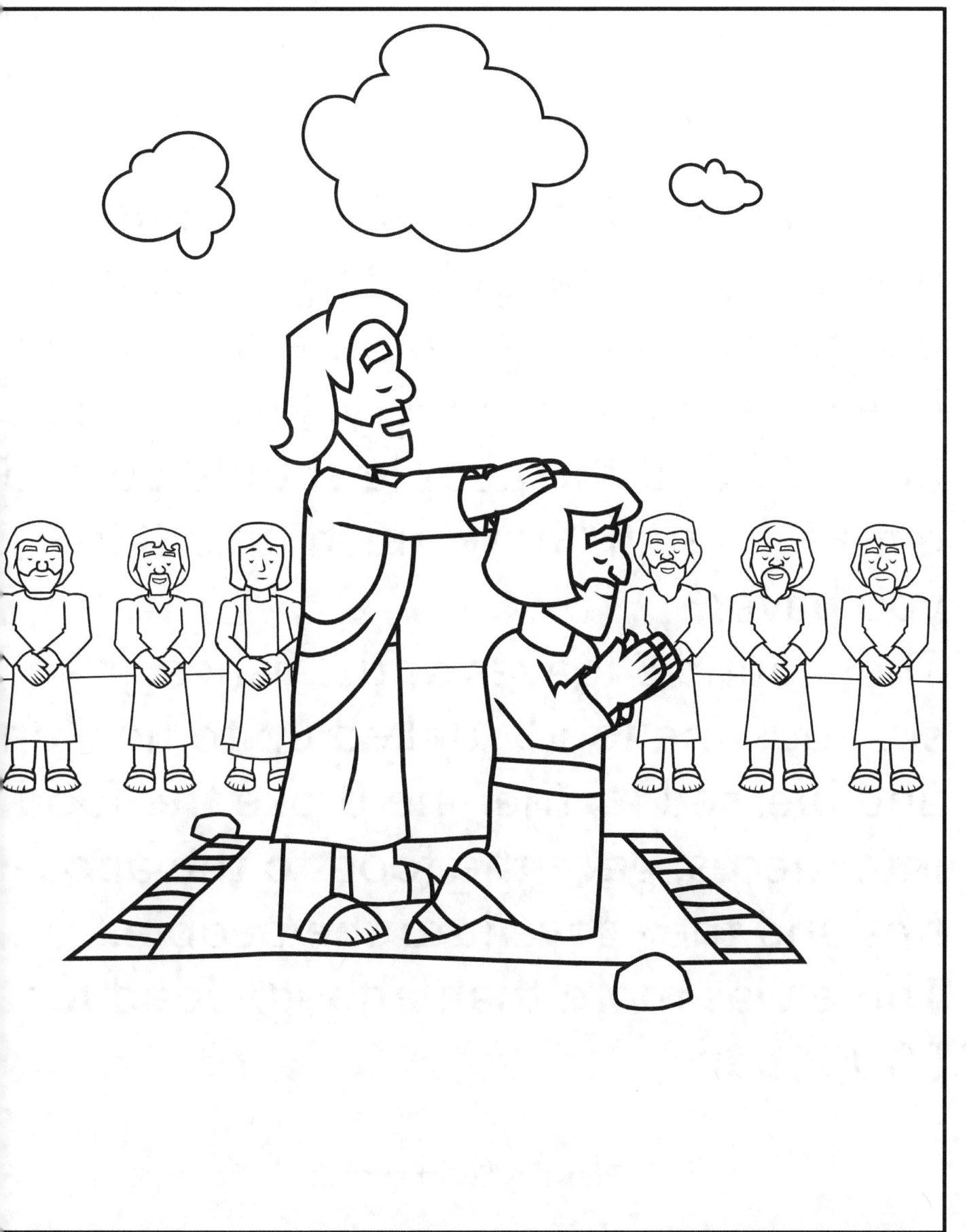

While the apostles were healing the sick, Jesus taught a large crowd of people many things. Before they knew it, everybody was hungry. Jesus' apostles said that the people should go and eat. Jesus said "how much bread do you have?"

They found 5 loaves and 2 fishes. Jesus took the food, looked up to heaven and blessed it. Then he broke the food into pieces, gave the food to the apostles and they gave it to the people. There was more than enough food for 5000 men.

Mark 6:34-44

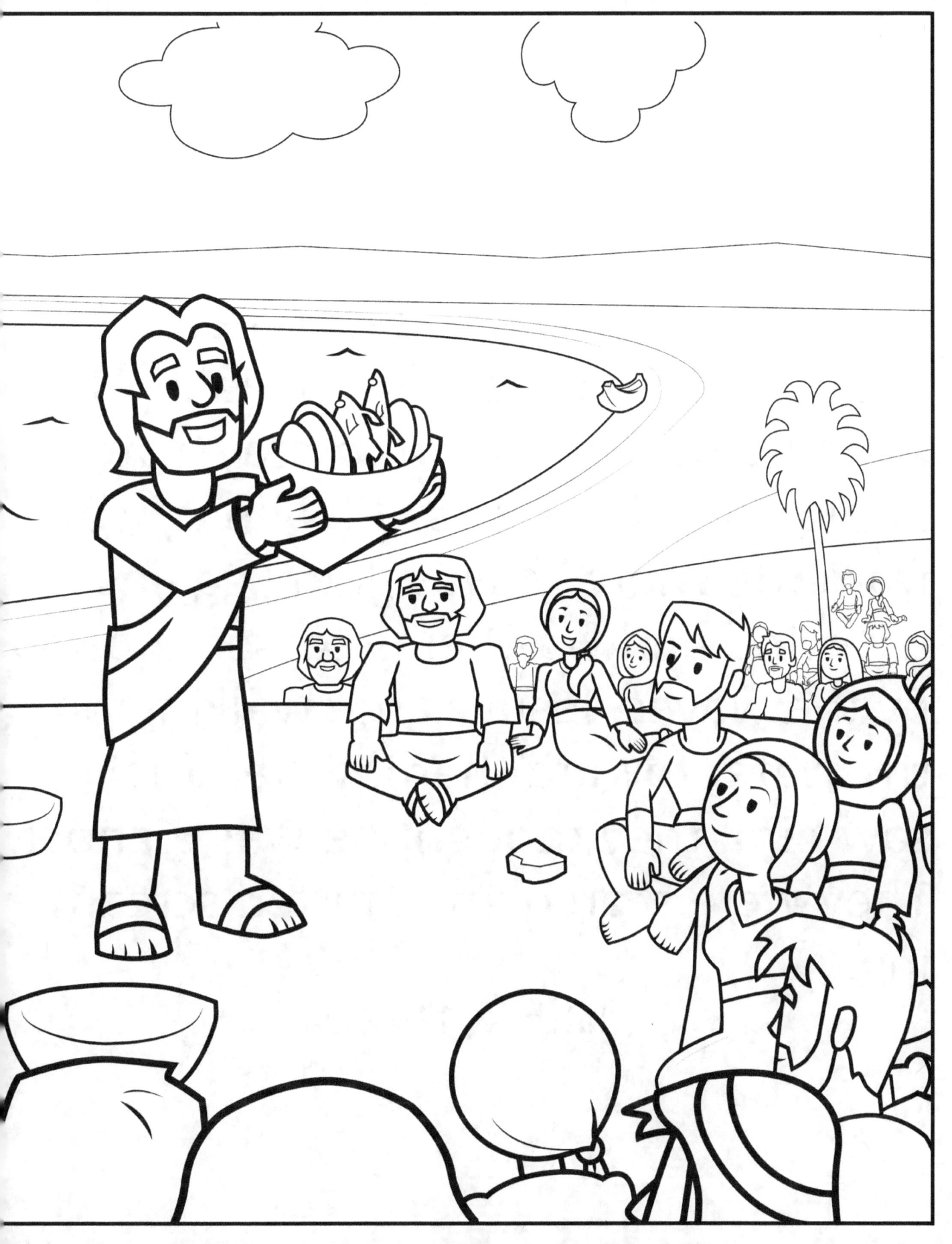

Jesus told his apostles to get in the boat and go back across the lake. He went up the mountain to pray. Late at night the boat was still a long way from the shore. It was going against the wind and was being tossed around by the waves. Jesus came walking on the water toward them. When they saw him, they thought he was a ghost. They were scared and started screaming.

Matthew 14:22-24

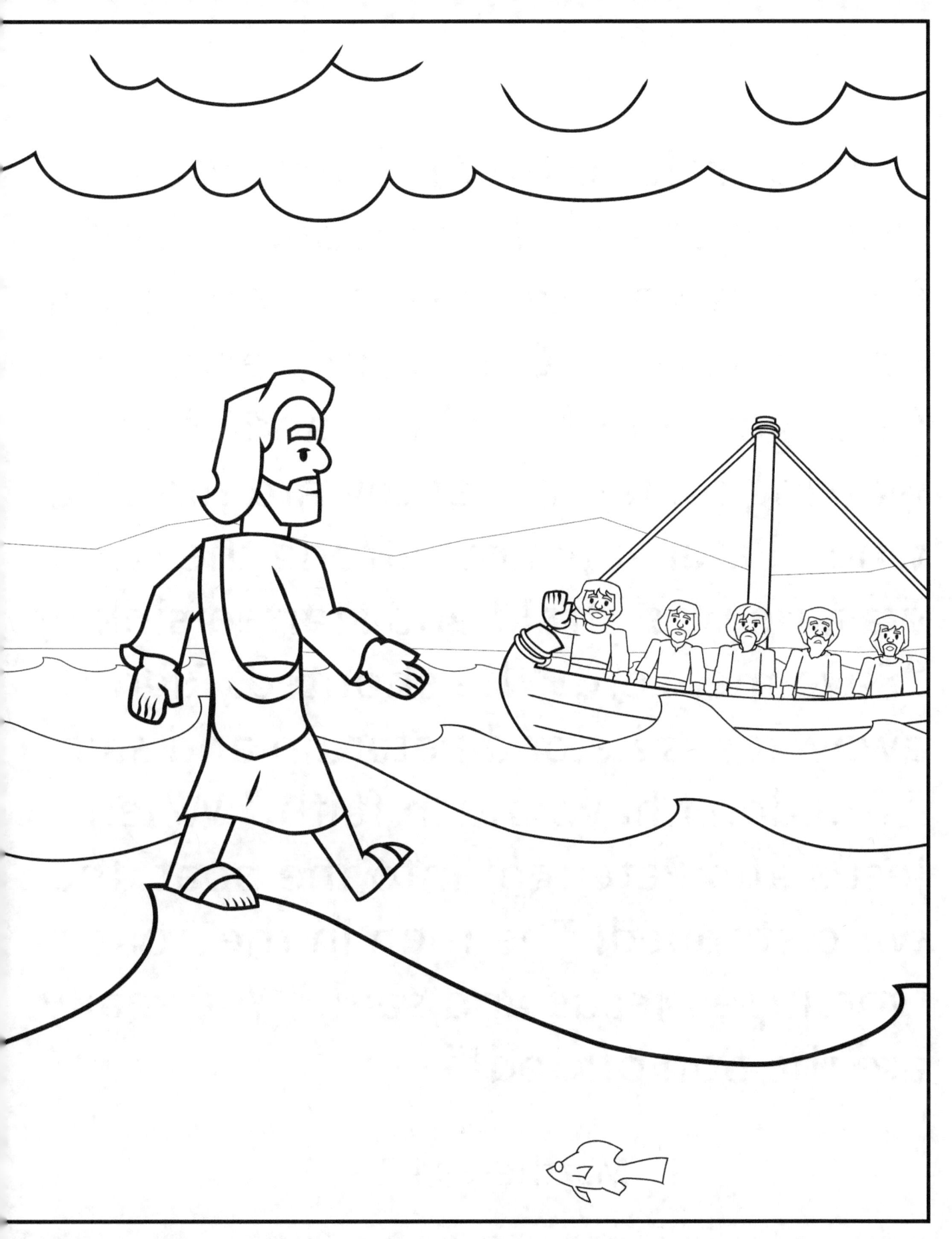

Jesus said to them, "I am Jesus. Don't be afraid." Peter replied, "Lord, if it is really you, tell me to come to you on the water." "Come on!" Jesus said. Peter got out of the boat and started walking on the water toward him. But when Peter saw how strong the wind was, he was afraid and started sinking. "Save me, Lord!" he shouted. Right away, Jesus helped Peter up and said, "You don't have much faith." When Jesus and Peter got into the boat, the wind stopped. The men in the boat worshiped Jesus and said, "You really are the Son of God!"

Matthew 14:27-33

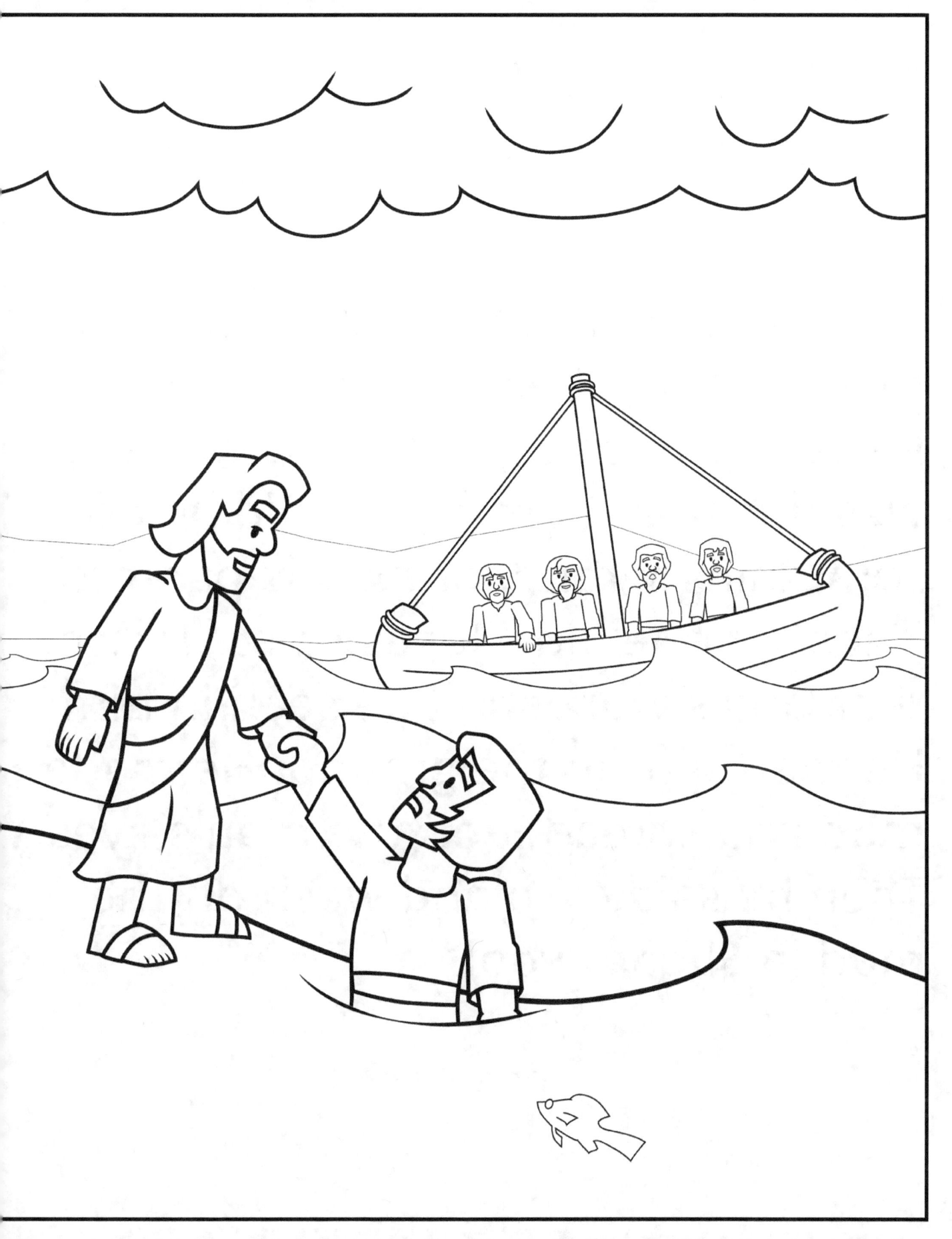

As Jesus walked along, he saw a man who had been blind since birth. Jesus' disciples asked, "Teacher, why was this man born blind? Did he do something wrong, or did his parents? "Neither one did." Jesus said. "It's so that God's work shall be seen in him." He then spit on the ground. He made mud and spread it on the man's eyes. Then he said, "Go and wash off the mud in Siloam Pool."

John 9:1-6

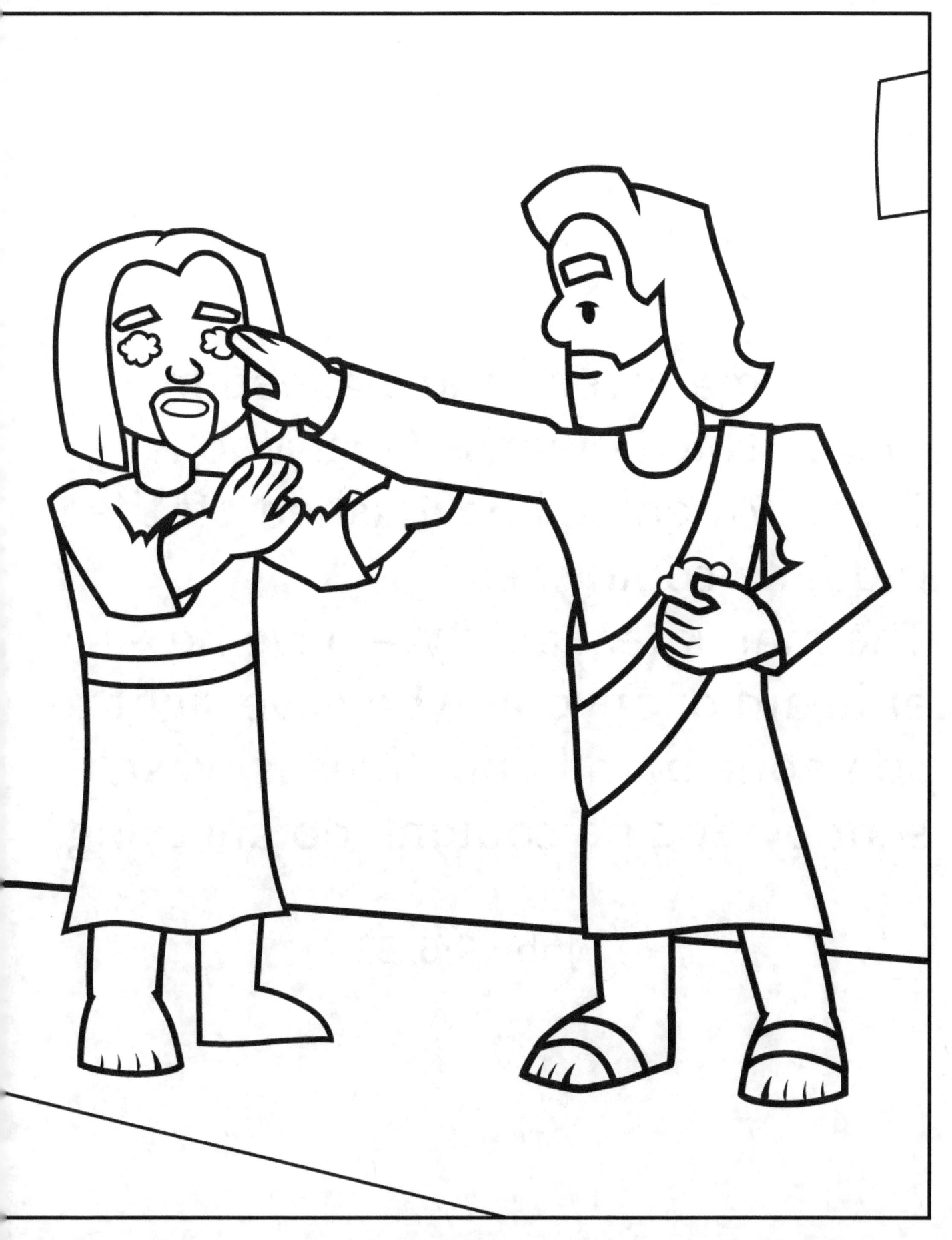

The man went and washed in Si-loam, which means "One Who Is Sent." When he had washed off the mud, he could see.
The man later said "We have never heard of anyone who gave sight to someone born blind. If Jesus wasn't sent by God he couldn't do anything."

John 9:6, 32

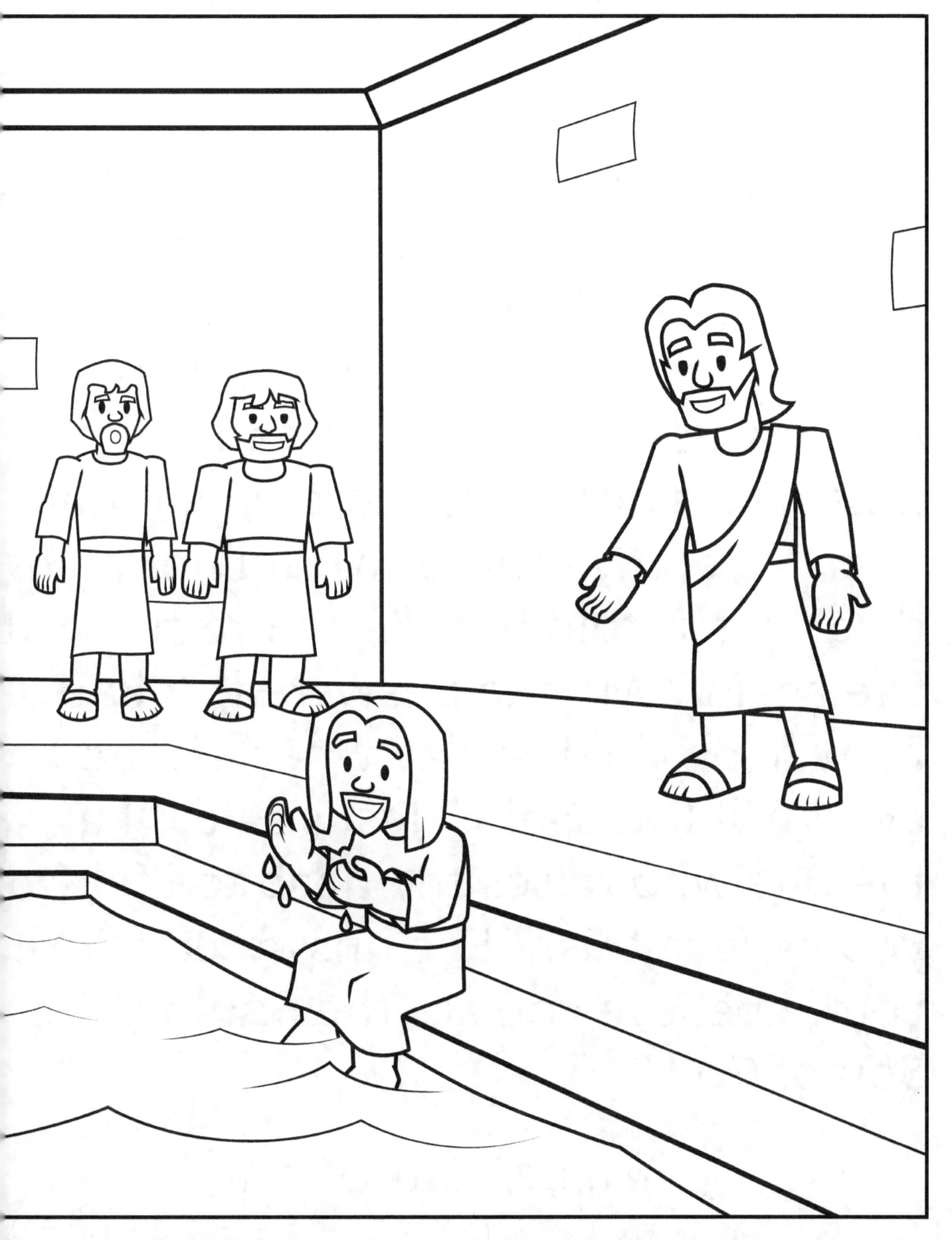

Lazarus had two sisters, Mary and Martha. They sent a message to Jesus to tell him that Lazarus was very sick. Jesus didn't go to help until 4 days after Lazarus had died. Martha went to meet Jesus and said, "Lord, if you had been here, my brother would not have died." Jesus told her, "Your brother will live again!" Martha answered, "I know he will on the last day when all the dead will live again." Jesus said, "I am the one who raises the dead to life! Do you believe this?" She answered, "Yes, Lord. I believe you are the **Savior**, the Son of God."

John 11:1, 3, 17, 20-21, 23-27

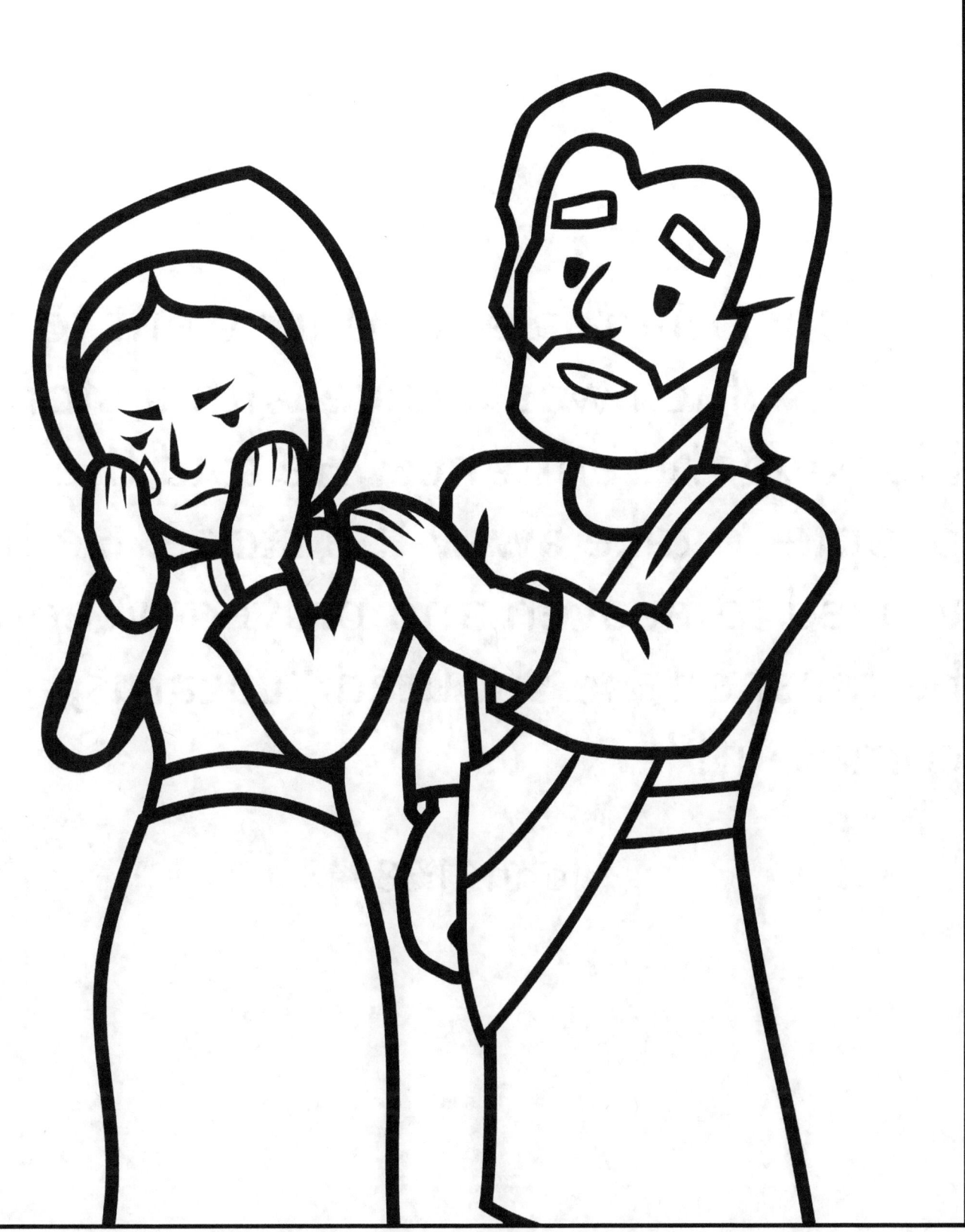

Jesus, Martha and Mary went to the tomb, which was a cave with a stone blocking the entrance. He told the people to take away the stone. He then looked to heaven and prayed. When he finished, he shouted "Lazarus, come out!"

John 11:38-43

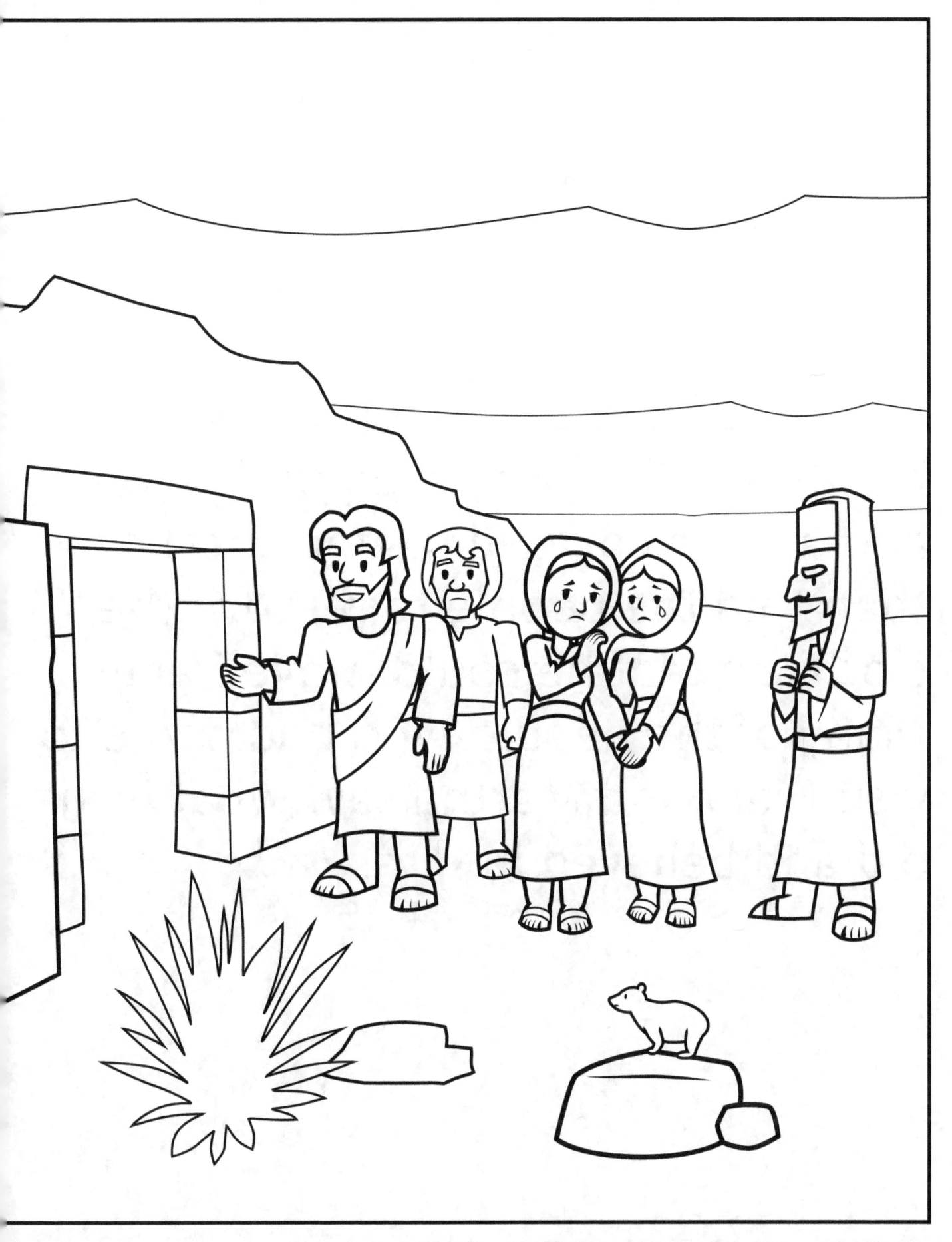

Lazarus came out of the cave. His hands and feet were tied up in cloth, and a cloth covered his face. Jesus then told the people to remove the cloths so that he could move freely. Many of the people who had come to visit Mary and Martha saw what Jesus did and believed in him.

John 11:44-45

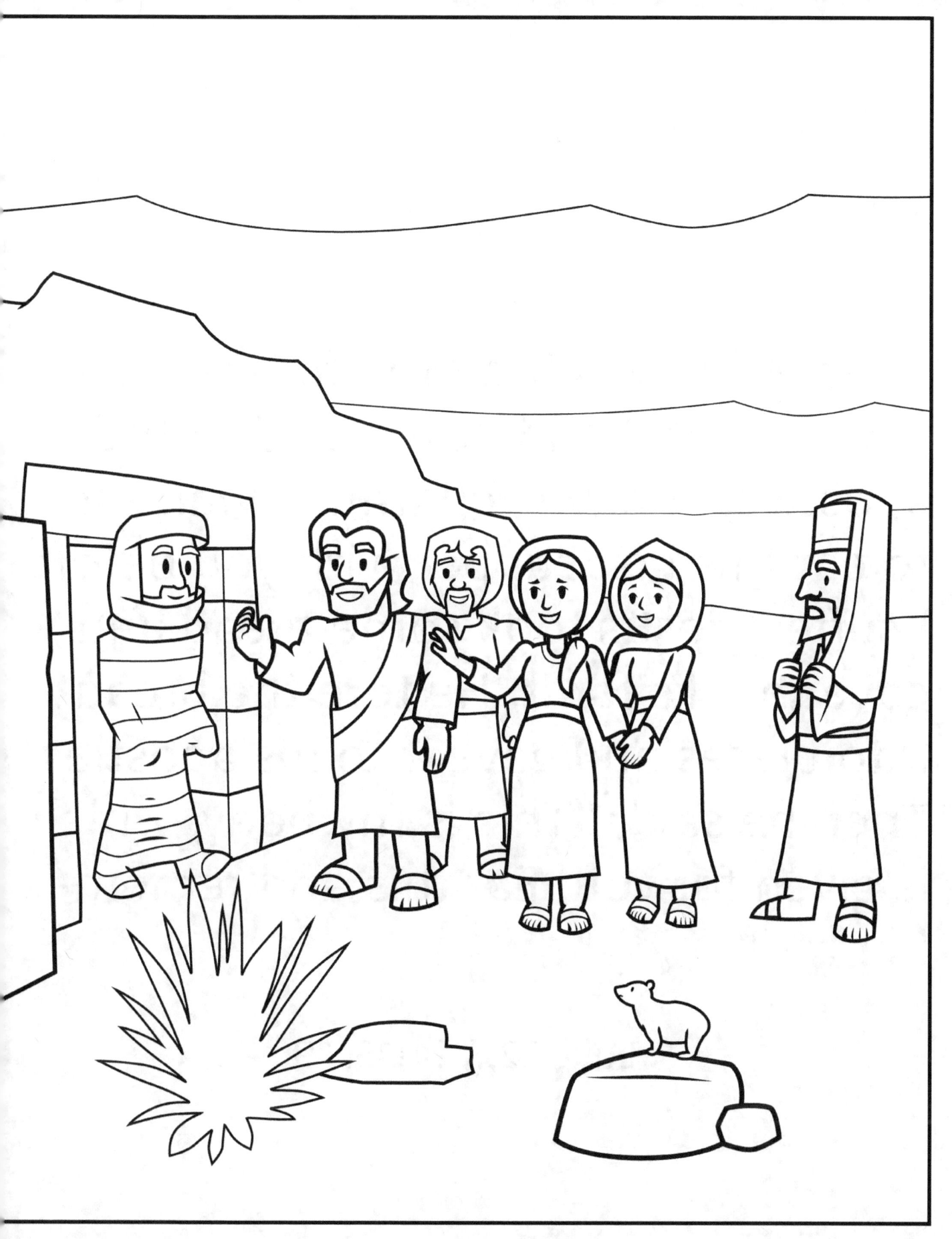

When it was the time for the Festival of Flat Bread, Jesus said to the apostles, "I have very much wanted to eat this last supper with you before I suffer." Jesus took some bread and gave thanks for it. He tore the bread into pieces and gave it to his apostles. Then he said, "This is my body, which is given for you. Eat this and remember me!"

Luke 22:7, 14–15, 19

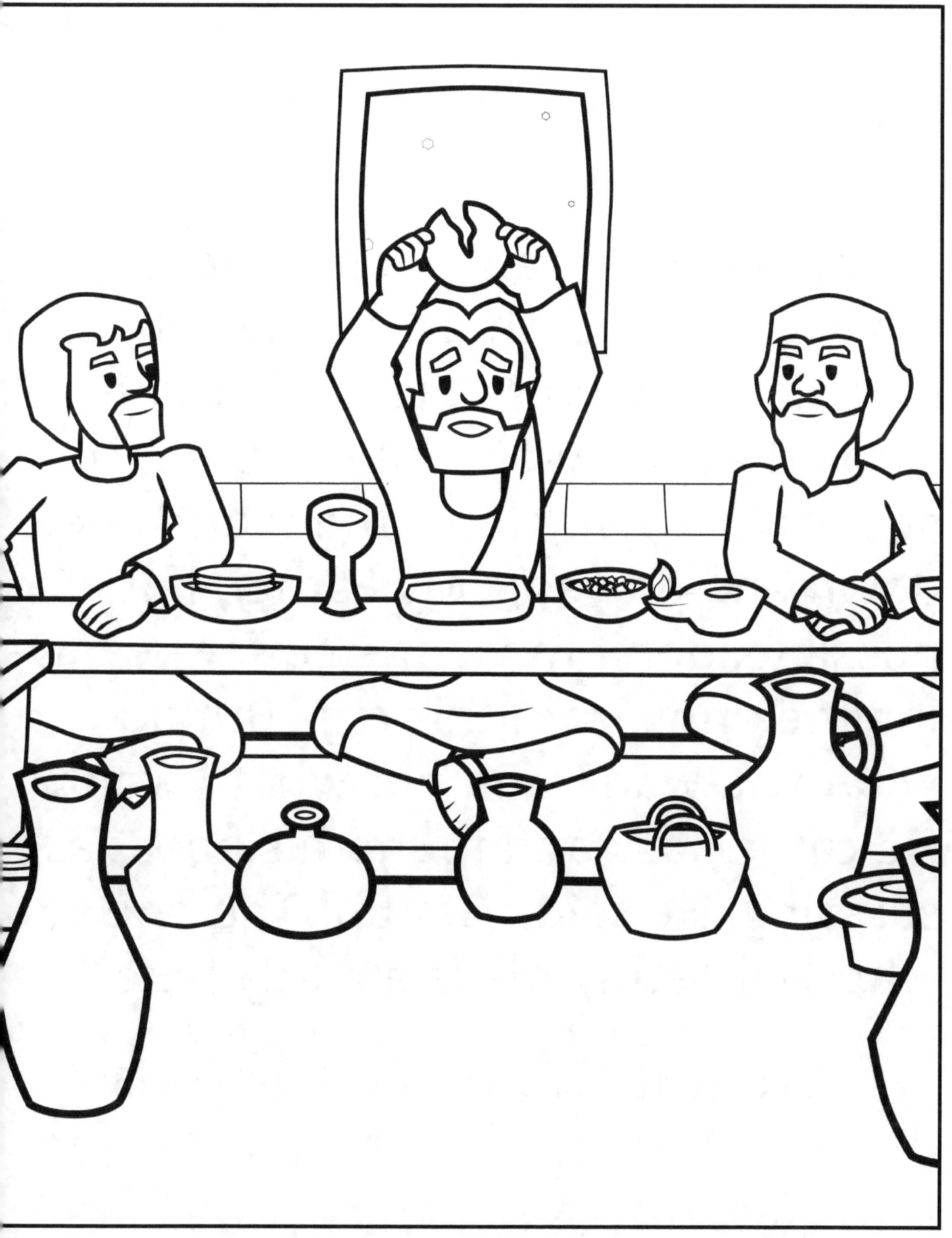

Jesus and the apostles went to a place called Gethsemane which means "Olive Press". Jesus told them "Pray that you won't be tempted." Jesus walked away from them and knelt down and prayed, "My Father, if it is possible, don't make me suffer by having me drink from this cup. But do what you want, and not what I want." He came back and found his apostles sleeping. He said "Get up! The one who will betray me is already here."

Luke 22:40; Matthew 26:36, 39, 45-46

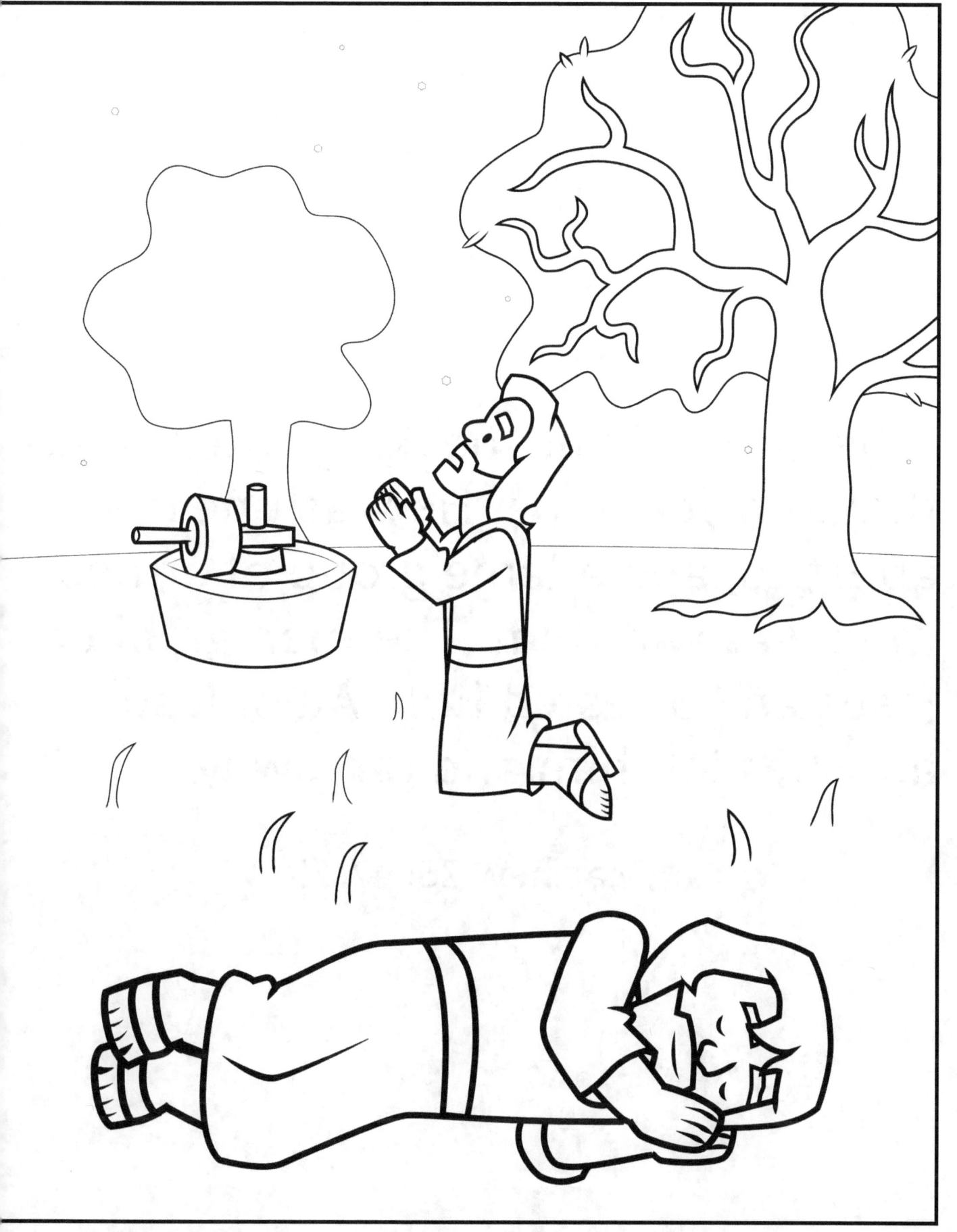

Jesus was still speaking when Judas the betrayer came. He was one of the apostles, and a large group of armed men was with him. The men grabbed Jesus and arrested him. All of Jesus' apostles left him and ran away.

Matthew 26: 47, 55

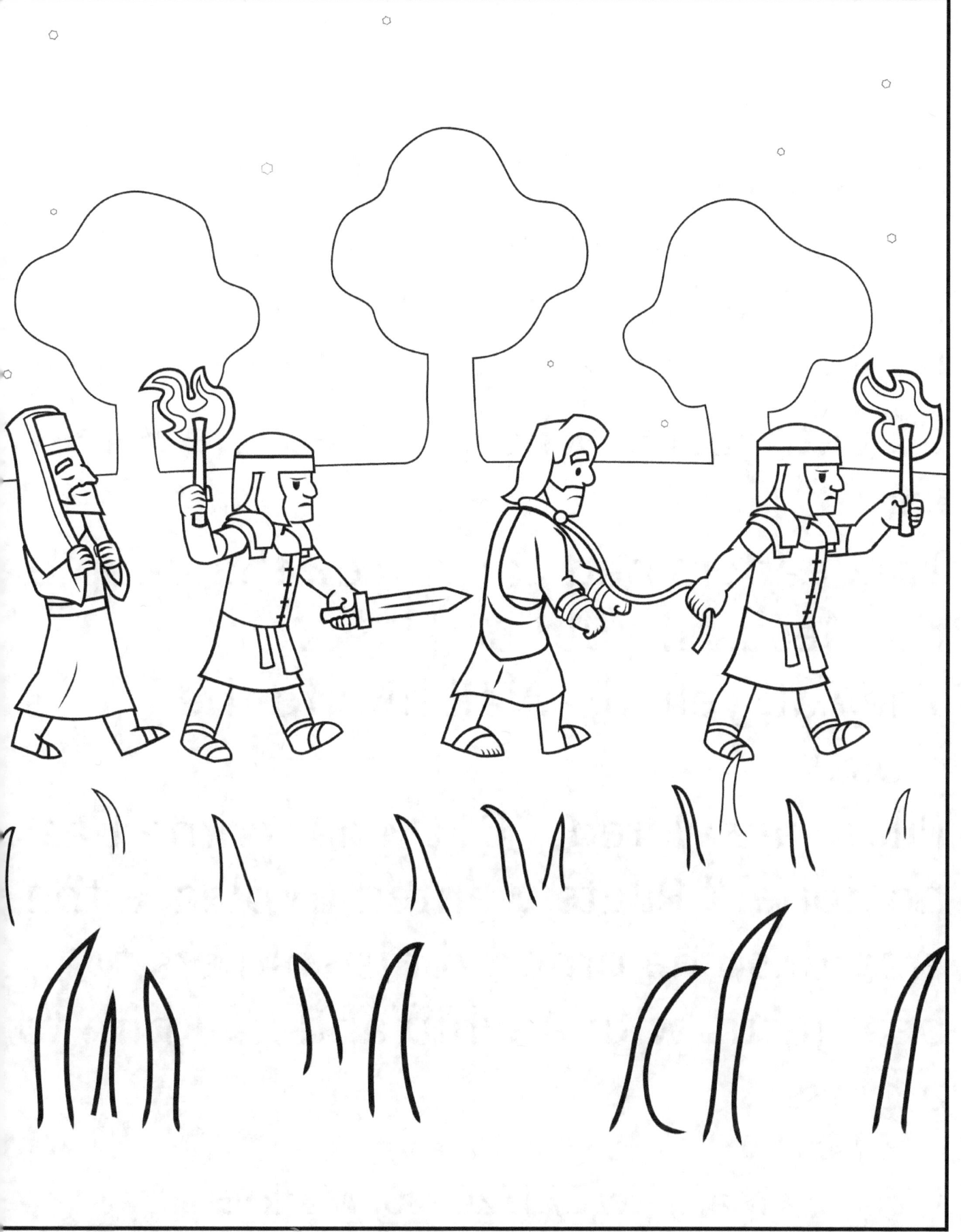

Early the next morning the nation's leaders met and decided that Jesus should be put to death. They tied him up and led him to Pilate the Governor. Pilate asked the crowd, "What am I to do with Jesus, who is called the **Savior**?"

The leaders had convinced the people that Jesus should be killed.

They all yelled, "Nail him to the cross!"

Pilate answered, "But what crime has he done?" Pilate wanted to please the crowd, so he ordered his soldiers to beat Jesus with a whip and nail him to a cross.

Matthew 27:1, 20-26; Mark 15:5

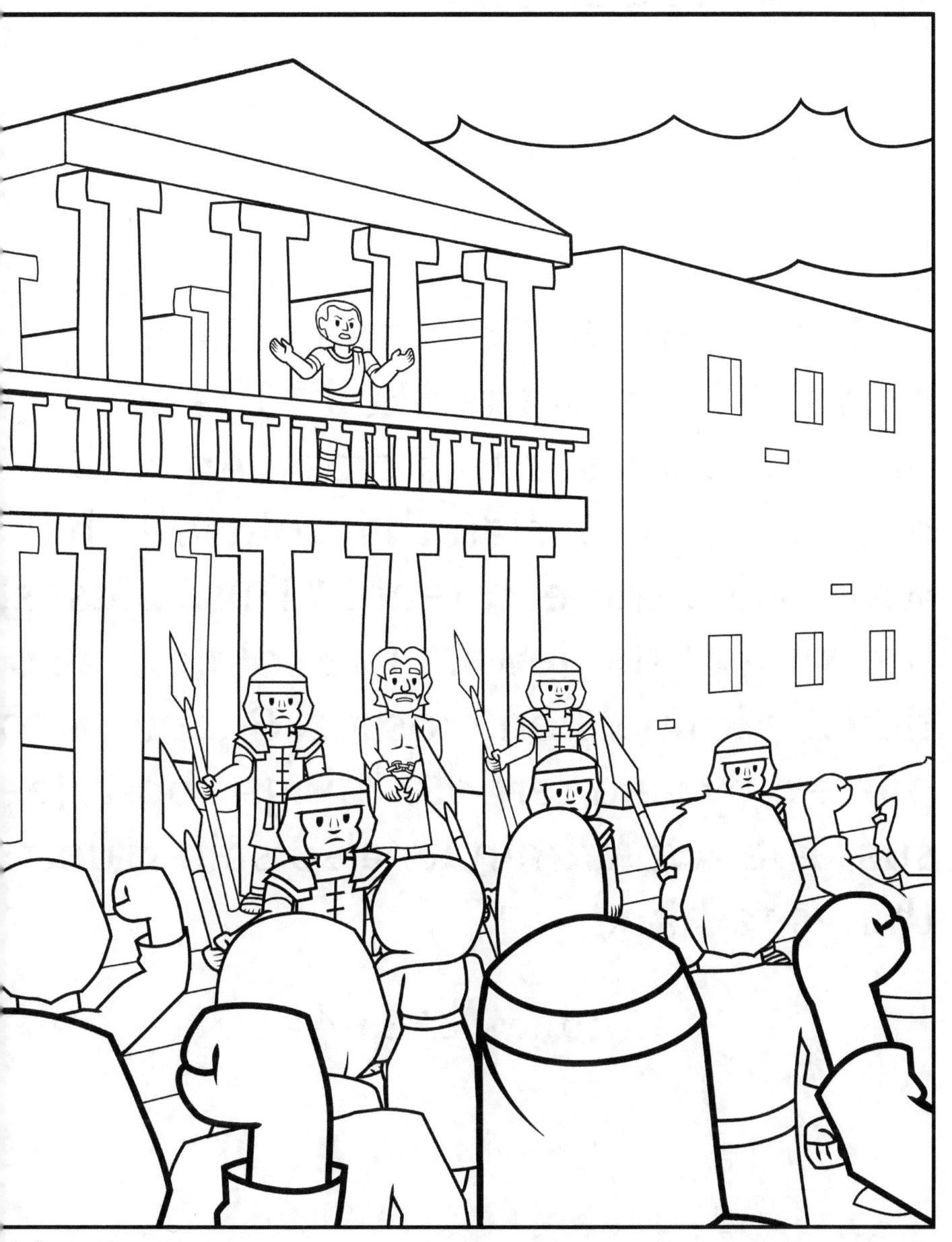

They came to Golgotha, which means "Place of the Skull". The soldiers nailed Jesus to a cross. Above his head they put a sign that told why he was nailed there. It read, "This is Jesus, the King of the Jews." The soldiers also tied 2 criminals on crosses. People who passed by said terrible things about Jesus. The two criminals also said cruel things to him.

Matthew 27: 33-44

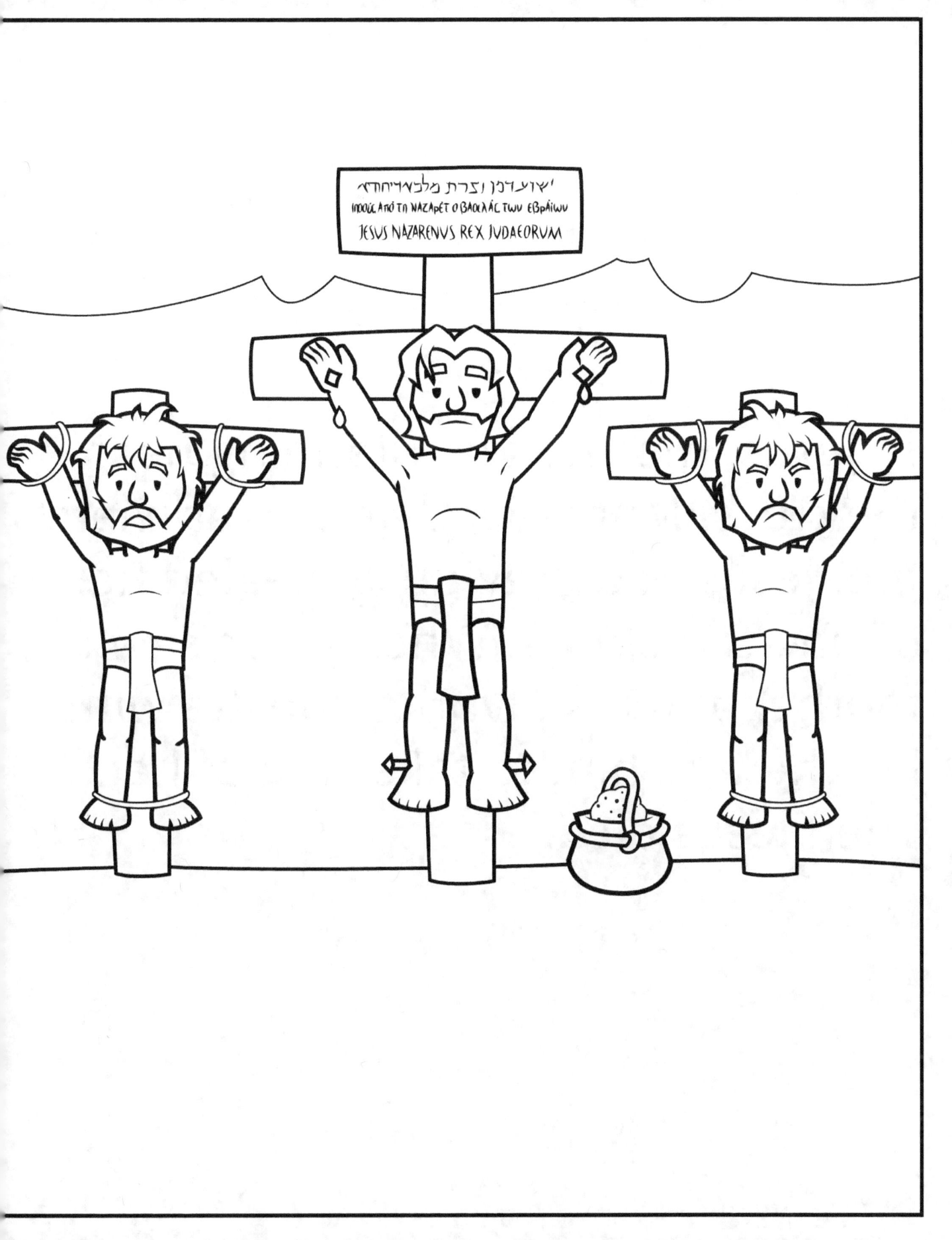

Jesus' mother was standing near the cross. Mary Magdalene was there too. Jesus had previously healed her of unclean spirits. When Jesus saw his mother and his favorite apostle with her, he told him to take care of her. Then Jesus died.

John 19:25-27, 30

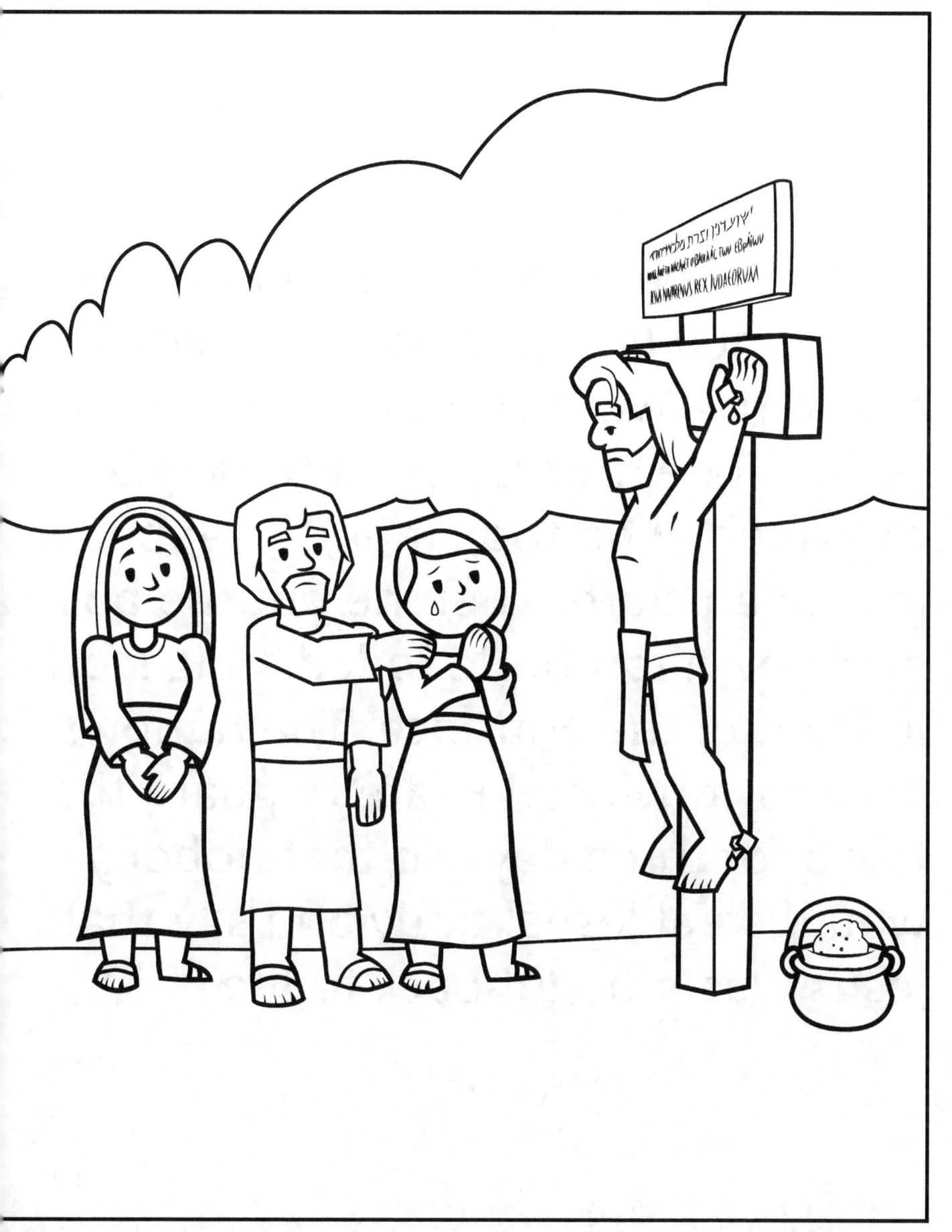

That evening a rich student of Jesus named Joseph from the town of Arithamea went and asked for Jesus' body. Pilate ordered for it to be given to Jospeh, who took it and wrapped it in a clean cloth. Then he put the body in his own tomb. He rolled a big stone in front of the entrance. The nation's leaders convinced Pilate to guard the tomb for three days so that nobody would steal Jesus' body and say that Jesus was brought back to life.

Matthew 27: 57-65

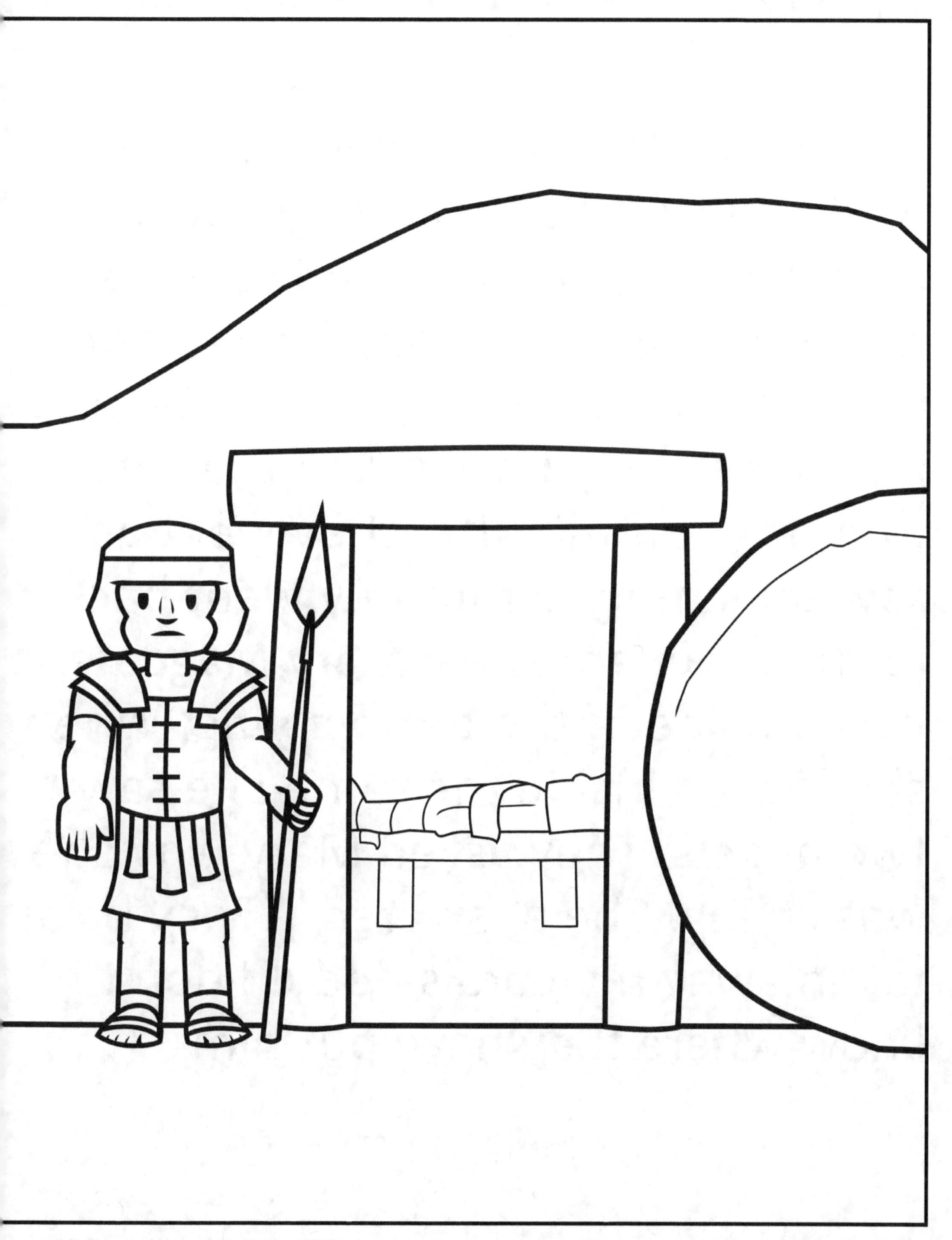

2 days later, on Sunday morning, while it was still dark, Mary Magdalene went to the tomb and saw that the stone had been rolled away from the entrance. She ran to tell Peter and John that "they have taken the Lord from the tomb!" After they went and saw the empty tomb they went back to the other apostles. Mary Magdalene was outside of the tomb crying. When she looked inside the tomb she saw two angels. They asked Mary why she was crying. She answered, "They have taken away my Lord's body! I don't know where they have put him."

John 20:1-13

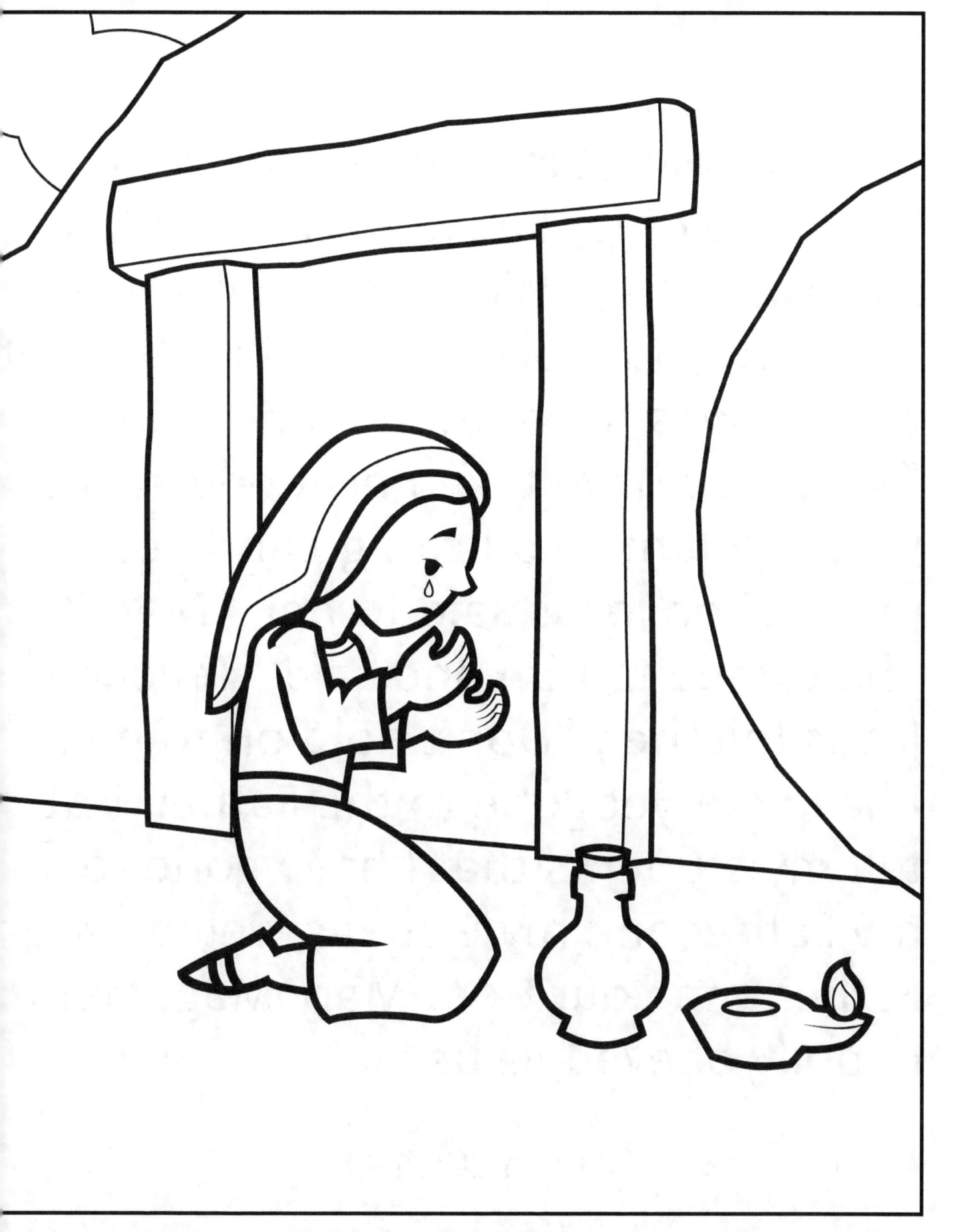

Jesus was standing behind Mary, but she did not know who he was. Jesus asked her, "Why are you crying? Who are you looking for?" She thought that he was the gardener and said, "Sir, if you have taken his body away, please tell me, so I can go and get him." Then Jesus said to her, "Mary!" She turned to him and said "Teacher." Jesus told her, "Don't hold on to me. I have not yet gone to the Father. But tell my students that I have gone to my Father and my God, as well as your Father and your God. Mary Magdalene happily obeyed Jesus.

John 20:14-18

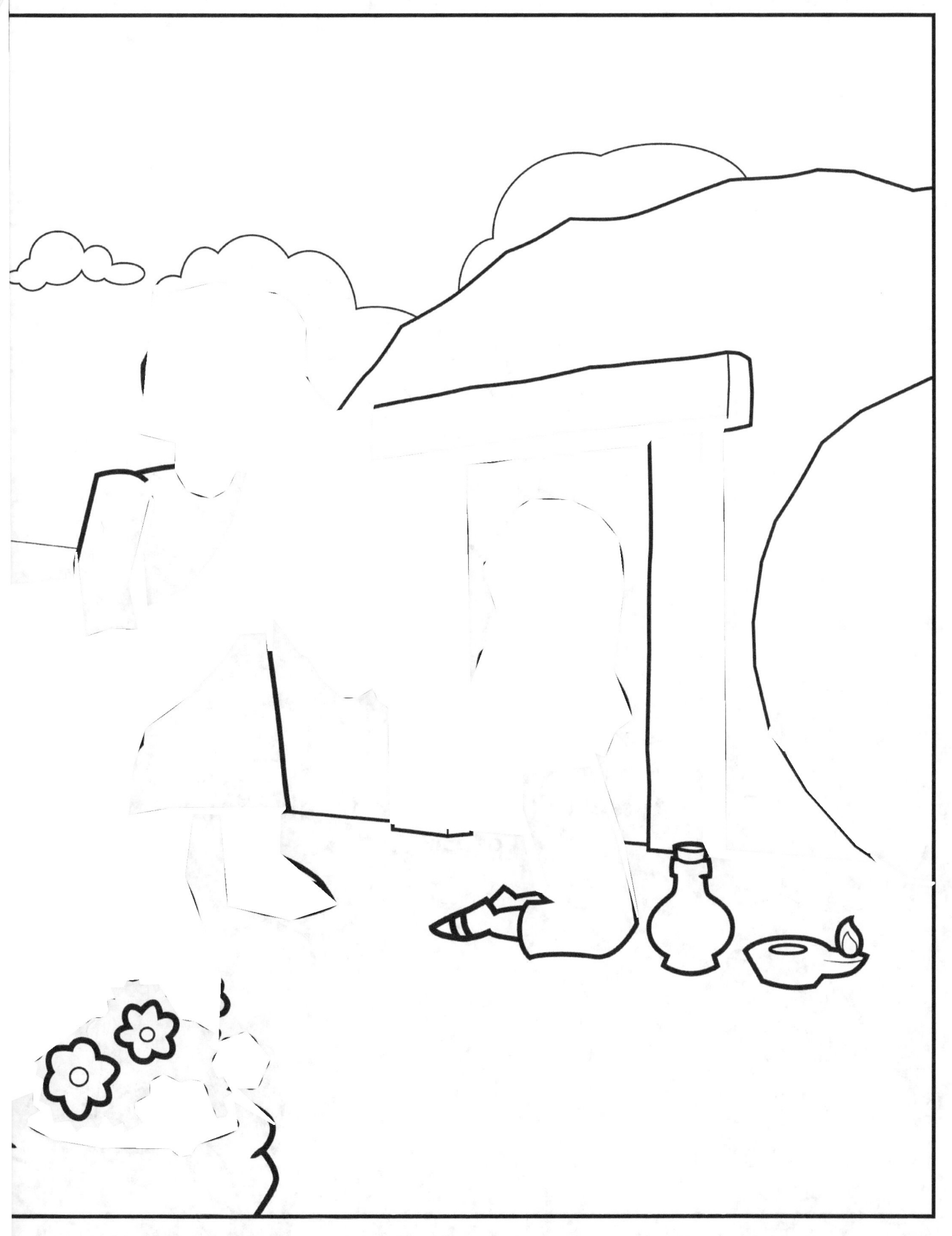

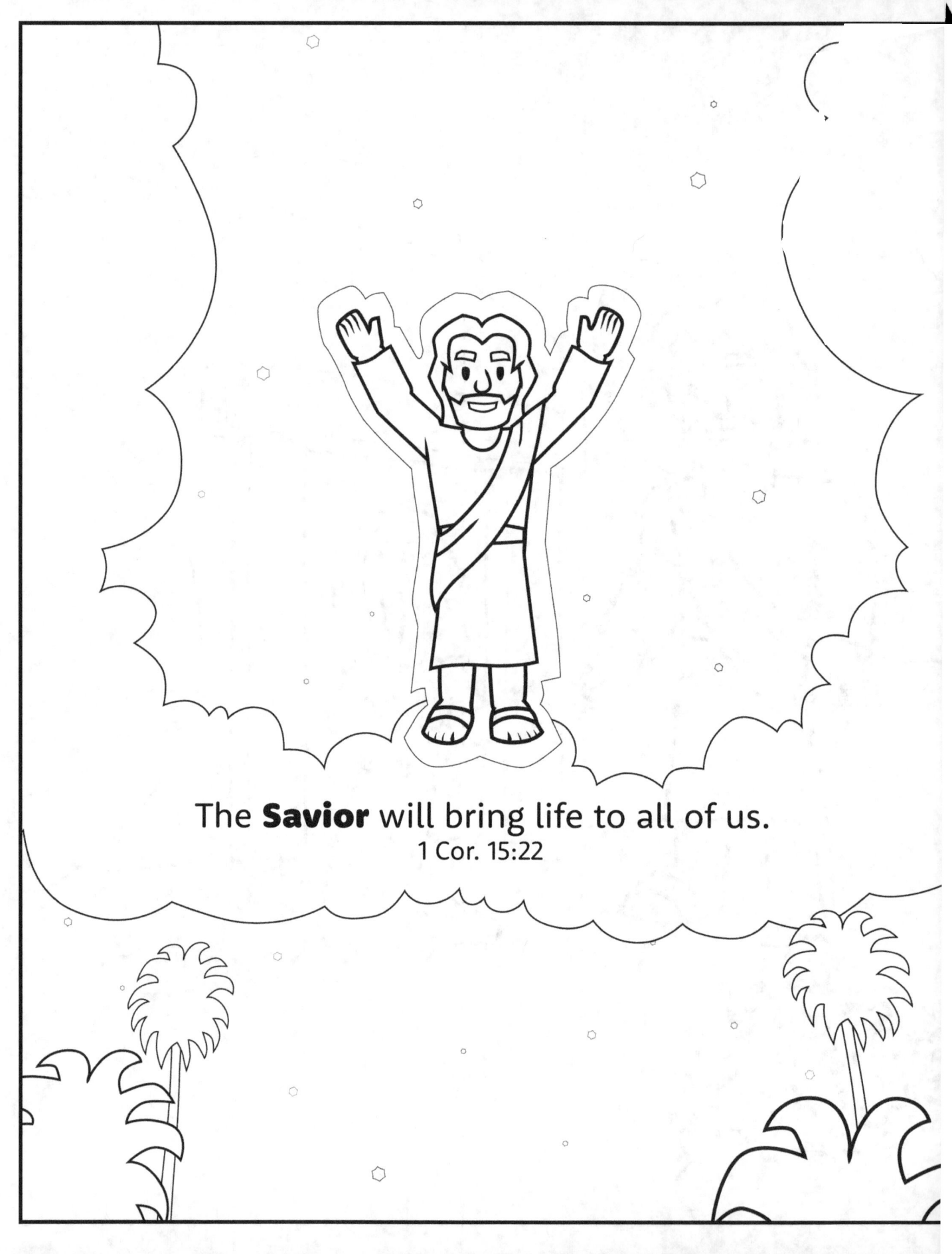

The **Savior** will bring life to all of us.
1 Cor. 15:22